HOCKEY SCIENCE

Shar Levine and
Leslie Johnstone

Winning Experiments

illustrations by
Lorenzo Del Bianco

SCHOLASTIC CANADA LTD.
Toronto New York London Auckland Sydney
Mexico City New Delhi Hong Kong Buenos Aires

Scholastic Canada Ltd.
604 King Street West, Toronto, Ontario M5V 1E1, Canada

Scholastic Inc.
557 Broadway, New York, NY 10012, USA

Scholastic Australia Pty Limited
PO Box 579, Gosford, NSW 2250, Australia

Scholastic New Zealand Limited
Private Bag 94407, Botany, Manukau 2163, New Zealand

Scholastic Children's Books
Euston House, 24 Eversholt Street, London NW1 1DB, UK

For Josh and Rachel. Mazel Tov!
—SL

For Chris and Emily.
—LJ

Acknowledgements
The authors are grateful for the assistance and technical advice of James Wendland, BHK, MHK, the senior exercise physiologist at Peak Centre for Human Performance.
Thank you for your time and help!

Library and Archives Canada Cataloguing in Publication

Levine, Shar, 1953-
Hockey science : 25 winning experiments / by Shar Levine and Leslie Johnstone ; illustrations by Lorenzo Del Bianco.

ISBN 978-1-4431-0777-8

1. Hockey--Experiments--Juvenile literature. I. Johnstone, Leslie II. Del Bianco, Lorenzo III. Title.

GV847.25.L48 2012 j796.962078 C2012-901666-7

6 5 4 3 2 1 Printed in Singapore 46 12 13 14 15 16

TABLE OF CONTENTS

INTRODUCTION

It's Saturday night and you're in front of your television ready to watch your favourite team take on their archrivals for a spot in the first round of the playoffs. The score is tied and there's less than a minute left in the game. The star forward grabs the puck and races down the ice on a breakaway, past centre, toward the opposition's net. You're on the edge of your seat, along with everyone at the arena. With a flick of his wrist, the puck goes in the top corner. Your team advances!

That goal isn't just about years of training and skill. Believe it or not, it also has everything to do with science.

State-of-the-art science goes into the materials that make the skates, sticks, pads and helmets. Trainers use high-tech equipment to analyze a player's balance, muscles and strength. Nutritionists work with coaches to create special meals or drinks that will keep athletes playing at their peak. And team doctors work with players' bodies and minds to improve performance.

Science goes into making the ice the players skate on, the shatterproof glass around the rink and the temperature of the puck.

This book might not make you a number one draft pick, but understanding the science behind hockey might make you a better player. Even if you're just a hockey fan, then this book will help you appreciate some of the science involved in your favourite sport.

SAFETY FIRST!

Playing hockey in the house is probably not a good idea. Here are some simple rules to keep in mind when trying the activities in *Hockey Science*. If you aren't sure if something is okay to do, ask an adult.

REMEMBER:

1. Ask a parent before trying any of these experiments.
2. Always wear appropriate safety equipment.
3. Tell an adult if you or anyone else has been hurt.
4. Read all the steps of the activity and gather your equipment before you begin. If you are unsure of how to do something, ask an adult.
5. Leave a safe distance between you and others when performing an activity.

NOTE TO PARENTS, TEACHERS AND COACHES

Not every child will play hockey in the Olympics or be drafted by the National Hockey League. But every child can learn something about the science in hockey. Maybe your child is destined to become a materials engineer and will invent a new kind of composite for hockey sticks. Or maybe your child will want to specialize in sports nutrition. If math is something that your child excels in, then there's no better place to start than hockey statistics or the geometry of where a goalie should stand to stop a slapshot. There's more to the sport of hockey than being a player. This book will help children make the connections between science, math and hockey.

Hockey can be an expensive and time-consuming sport. The activities in this book, however, won't cost you much, and they won't take long to perform. Even if kids don't own hockey equipment or have access to ice time, they can still try the experiments. So here are some ways kids can use science to improve their game or to simply appreciate how a pro makes it look so easy to score a goal or block a shot.

It's game time!

1 PUMPING UP THE ICE

Many people argue about where hockey was first played in Canada. Was it Windsor, Nova Scotia? Kingston, Ontario? Montreal, Quebec? Or somewhere else? No matter where it got its start, it was first played outdoors. But since the early 1900s, people have been playing hockey on indoor rinks. Refrigeration makes this possible even in cities where it never gets cold enough to form ice. How does it work?

You Will Need

- a helper
- a bicycle pump

What to Do

1. Fill the bicycle pump with air and then place your thumb over the outlet of the bicycle pump. Touch the cylinder of the pump to test its temperature.
2. Have your helper push down on the plunger of the pump. Feel the cylinder. Does the temperature change?
3. Have your helper empty the bicycle pump of air. Place your thumb over the outlet of the pump. What happens to the temperature of the cylinder when you try to fill the sealed pump with air?

WHAT HAPPENED?

When you pushed down, the air inside the bicycle pump heated up. When you tried to pull up on the sealed pump, it caused the small amount of air inside to expand and cool down. Compressing gas makes it get hotter. Gas gets cold as it expands. This principle is used in the refrigeration system at the ice rink to take heat from under the ice and move it away, outside the building. Ice rinks compress ammonia gas, which heats up and sheds its heat outside. Then, back inside, the ammonia is made to rapidly expand so it gets very cold, just like when you pulled up on the bicycle pump. The cold ammonia is used to pull heat from another liquid, usually brine or ethylene glycol, which is pumped through pipes in the concrete floor under the ice to keep it cool. The ammonia is then compressed again and heats up to repeat the cycle.

2 ON THE LINE

Everyone likes to see the Zamboni hit the ice, but have you ever wondered why it doesn't smudge the lines? Let's look at what happens when you try to paint on ice.

You Will Need

- 3 recipe cards
- a small can of latex paint
- a paintbrush
- an ice cube
- a small container
- a refrigerator and freezer
- a disposable waterproof container such as a margarine container
- water
- a paper towel

What to Do

1. Paint a small circle in the centre of each of the three recipe cards.
2. Place an ice cube in the small container and paint the top of the ice cube with the latex paint.
3. Place one card and the container with the ice cube in the freezer.
4. Place the second card in the refrigerator.
5. Place the third card somewhere where it will remain undisturbed at room temperature for about 2 hours.
6. After 2 hours, fill the disposable waterproof container three-quarters full of warm tap water. Dip each of your samples into the water and look at what happens to the paint. Wipe the top of the ice cube with a dry paper towel.

WHAT HAPPENED?

You were able to paint the ice cube, but the paint wiped off easily with the paper towel. When you dipped the cards that were left in the freezer and the refrigerator in the warm water, the paint came off. But the paint stayed on the card that was left at room temperature. That's because latex paint doesn't dry properly at low temperatures. Ice rinks use special paint that hardens in the cold and keeps the lines in place when water is sprayed on top.

3 SLIP SLIDING AWAY

Do you think hockey is cool? Of course you do! And so does the NHL. They've called it "the coolest game on Earth." But it could also be called the fastest game. On any surface other than ice, hockey wouldn't be as fast. Why not? Let's find out.

You Will Need

- an adult helper
- a long, thick rubber band
- a ruler with a hole in one end
- a small block of wood approximately 10 x 10 x 5 cm (4 x 4 x 2 in)
- a finishing nail that is 4 cm (1.6 in) long
- a hammer
- a board about 45 cm (18 in) long
- several books
- masking tape
- aluminum foil
- sandpaper
- a pencil
- paper

What to Do

1. Push one end of a rubber band through the hole in a ruler to make a small loop on one side of the ruler. Take the other end of the rubber band and push it through the loop. Pull gently to secure the rubber band to the ruler.
2. Have an adult hammer a nail into one side of the small block of wood. Part of the nail should stick out. Have the adult tap on the side of the nail to make the nail into a hook. Slip the loose end of your rubber band over the hook so that the rubber band can be used to pull the block.
3. Place one end of the long board on top of a stack of books to make a ramp. Try pulling the block up the ramp using the rubber band. Using the ruler, have your helper measure how far the band stretched to pull the block up the ramp. Record it on your paper.
4. Now cover the ramp with aluminum foil, taping it in place if needed. Try pulling the block up the foil-covered ramp. Record the result on your paper.
5. Remove the foil and cover the ramp with sandpaper, taping it in place. Try pulling the block up the ramp. Record your findings. Which surface stretched the rubber band the most?

WHAT HAPPENED?

When the block was pulled up the wood and aluminum surfaces, the band stretched by the same amount, meaning it took about the same amount of **force**. This type of force is called tension force. Pulling the block up the sandpaper-covered ramp stretched the band much further. If you were able to construct an ice-covered ramp you would have found the block much easier to pull. That's because ice and wood create less **friction** than sandpaper. And that's why players are able to move faster on ice!

COOL FACTS

Friction is a resistance to motion. Surfaces that allow objects to glide along them easily, such as ice, have very little friction. The less friction there is, the less **energy** it takes to travel across the surface.

4 FAST ICE, SLOW ICE

Okay, so we know that it's easier to play hockey on ice because of its smooth surface compared to other surfaces. But is all ice the same? How does it feel skating across the ice after the Zamboni has cleared it? How about by the end of the first period? It turns out that the surface of the ice can change at different temperatures or if the ice has been skated on and carved up by blades.

You Will Need

- a cookie sheet (one that fits into your freezer)
- water
- a cup
- a freezer
- a large nail
- 2 quarters or other large coins

What to Do

1. Place the cookie sheet into your freezer, making sure it is level and stable. Slowly fill the cookie sheet by pouring in cups of water. Place the quarters or other large coins in the freezer. Allow the water and the coins to cool overnight.
2. The next day, remove the cookie sheet from the freezer. Use a nail to scratch a line along the length of the ice so that it separates it into two halves.
3. Use the nail to scratch up one half, leaving the other side smooth. Remove any stray shavings of ice from the smooth side with your finger or a spatula.
4. Remove one coin from the freezer. Place it at one end of the smooth section of the ice and flick it with your finger to make it slide along the ice. How far does it go?
5. Remove the second quarter from the freezer. Place it at the end of the rough section of the ice and flick it with your finger. How far does it go?

WHAT HAPPENED?

You were able to flick the coin farther on the smooth ice surface than on the rough one. When you scratched up the ice with the nail, you made the surface bumpier and this increased the friction between the ice and the coin. You may also have noticed that the coin moved more slowly as the coin and the ice warmed up. A thin layer of water on the surface of the ice increased the friction between the coin and the ice and caused the coin to slow down or stick to the ice.

COOL FACTS

Have you ever heard someone say that hockey players prefer "cold ice"? Isn't all ice cold? Not always. In hotter climates, warm air can enter the arena when people come and go, warming up the ice. This means that it gets carved up easier. Canadian rinks such as Rexall Place in Edmonton, Alberta, are known for their fast ice because the colder the ice, the harder it is, and in winter, Edmonton is *cold*.

5 THE LONG AND THE SHORT OF IT

Can you imagine what would happen if an NHL star wore figure skates to play in a game? Other than looking a bit out of place, he'd probably trip over the toe picks at the front of his skates. What difference do certain types of skates make on the ice?

You Will Need

- different types of skates, such as figure skates, speed skates, hockey skates and goalie skates, or pictures of these skates
- a library card or other laminated card
- a large coin
- plush carpet
- a protractor

What to Do

1. Look carefully at the blades of different types of skates. Notice the length of the blade, the curve of the front and back of the blade and the shape of the bottom surface of the blade. If you don't have the actual skates to look at, you can look at photos to compare the shape of the blades or visit a sports store that sells different kinds of skates.
2. Hold a laminated card between your fingers so that the long edge of the card sticks out between your fingers. Slide the card in a straight line along a carpet.
3. Try sliding the card sideways along the carpet. Try turning the card in a series of small S-shaped turns.
4. Use a large coin instead of the card. Is it easier to turn and slide?
5. Use a protractor to measure the sharpest angle the card and coin can turn on the thick carpet.

WHAT HAPPENED?

The longer surface of the card made it harder to turn compared to the coin but easier to move in a straight line. The length and curved shape of skate blades are different depending on what skaters need to do. Speed skates have long, straight blades that make it easier to glide quickly along the ice but don't allow for turning and spinning. Figure skates and hockey skates have shorter, curved or slightly rounded blades that make it possible to make sharp turns because there is less contact with the surface. The jagged picks at the front of figure skate blades can be used to grip the ice and walk forward. Goalie skates have blades that are slightly flatter and longer than other hockey skates. This helps the goalie to balance better and move from side to side.

COOL FACTS

Archaeologists have discovered that ancient peoples made skates out of animal bones over 5,000 years ago. These skates were not used for sport; they were used for transportation over icy surfaces. Scientists have found bone skates in several places in central and northern Europe.

HEAD CASE

Have you ever been hit with a puck? It hurts. Can you imagine a time when hockey players *didn't* wear safety equipment? Protecting your head is especially important so that you don't get severe injuries such as **concussions.** Although the first helmet in the NHL dates back to the late 1920s, they did not become required gear until 1979. Let's take a look at how helmets protect our heads.

You Will Need

- bubble wrap
- 3 uncooked eggs
- tissue paper
- masking tape
- scissors
- a small, sealable plastic container slightly larger than an egg
- yogurt or pudding

What to Do

1. Wrap an uncooked egg with several layers of bubble wrap and use masking tape to hold the wrap in place. You can make this as large as you like. Be gentle!
2. Wrap a second egg with several layers of tissue paper and use masking tape to hold the wrap in place.
3. Put some yogurt or pudding into the container, then place the egg into it. Fill the container with yogurt or pudding so the egg is completely covered. Seal the container.
4. Go outside to a flat spot and hold each egg in its "helmet" at waist level. Drop the eggs. Which egg survived the crash?

NOTE: Make sure you wash your hands after handling raw eggs. Do not eat the yogurt or pudding.

WHAT HAPPENED?

You learned how different materials worked in protecting the egg. The helmet made from the bubble wrap protected the egg the best. That's because air pockets in the bubble wrap acted as a cushion, which absorbed the impact. Other materials may not have worked as well in keeping your eggs intact, as they absorbed less of the force from the fall. Hockey helmets include a protective shell with a foam padding filled with tiny air pockets that acts like the bubble wrap to absorb force. They absorb the force of falls or collisions and reduce the amount of damage that can be done to your brain. They also spread the force out over a larger area, decreasing the chances of cracking your skull. This reduces concussions and brain injuries that can cause long-term brain damage or even death.

COOL FACTS

The first NHL goaltender to wear a mask on a regular basis was Jacques Plante. At first legendary NHL coach Toe Blake wasn't too happy about it, but when Plante proved that he could not only play safer, but also play better in a mask, it became a permanent part of his equipment.

7 BEND AND FLEX

The game has gone into overtime with the minutes ticking away. The Canucks are playing the Flames. Daniel Sedin of the Canucks is positioned in front of the net. He takes a pass, takes the shot and . . . his stick breaks, spreading across the ice. We've all seen something like this happen in a game. Was it a bad stick? Why does this happen? Let science do the explaining.

You Will Need

- a helper
- a metre stick
- a tabletop or other firm surface
- a penny or other small coin

What to Do

1. Place a metre stick on a tabletop so that 10 cm (4 in) is hanging over the edge.

2. Have your helper hold the far end of the stick firmly on the table.
3. Push down gently on the end of the stick hanging over the edge. Can you flex the metre stick slightly?
4. Slide the metre stick so that 20 cm (8 in) of it is hanging over the edge. Have your helper hold the stick and try flexing it again. Do this again for 30 cm (12 in) and 40 cm (16 in). What happens when more of the stick can flex?
5. Slide the stick back so that 30 cm (12 in) of the stick overhangs the edge of the table. With your helper keeping the stick from moving, flex the stick gently and place a penny on the free end. Let go and watch the penny. Try this again but put more flex on the stick. See how high you can make the penny go, but be careful not to break the stick.

WHAT HAPPENED?

When you moved more of the stick off the tabletop, you were able to bend it easily. That's because wood is slightly flexible. When you put the penny on the end of the stick, flexed the stick a little bit and let go, the wood sprang back up and flicked the penny. Flexing the stick gave it some stored or **potential energy**. You released the energy when you let go. Flexing the ruler more stores more energy, so a larger flex made the penny go farther. Exerting too much force will cause the stick to snap in two as the wood doesn't have enough tensile strength (the amount of force the stick can take before breaking). Hockey sticks are made to handle much larger forces than a metre stick. They can be made of wood, but today players use **composite** sticks made of layers of materials such as fibreglass, carbon fibre and Kevlar.

COOL FACTS

Young players shouldn't use the stiff sticks used by NHL players. If a stick is too stiff, you won't be able to flex it and your shots will be weaker. A stick that is too flexible will bend too much and store less energy. Shortening a stick will make it less flexible, just like shortening the bendable part of the metre stick did in this experiment.

THAT'S A WRAP

After looking long and hard and trying out several sticks, you've finally decided on the one you want. It's perfect, right? So then why do you go home and tape it? If cutting down on friction is important (see pages 8–9), wouldn't the tape create more friction?

You Will Need

- a wooden ruler
- hockey tape
- a street hockey or ice hockey puck
- a wooden floor or other smooth surface
- a pillow

What to Do

1. Find a smooth surface, and clear a space so you won't hit anything when you perform this activity. Place a large pillow about 1.5 m (5 ft) away from you. This is your net.
2. Place the hockey puck on the floor and use the side of your ruler to gently shoot the puck toward the net. How easy is it to control the direction of the puck?
3. Wrap the ruler with hockey tape. Try step 2 again, this time with the wrapped ruler. Is it easier to control the direction of the puck this time?

WHAT HAPPENED?

You were able to control the puck more easily with the taped stick. Friction is a good thing in certain instances. If it weren't for friction, a puck would fly off a smooth hockey stick and the player would not be able to control the puck to send it where he or she wanted it to go. In many sports, players need to use friction to their advantage. Gymnasts use something called rosin or chalk on their hands to help them hold onto the bars or rings.

COOL FACTS

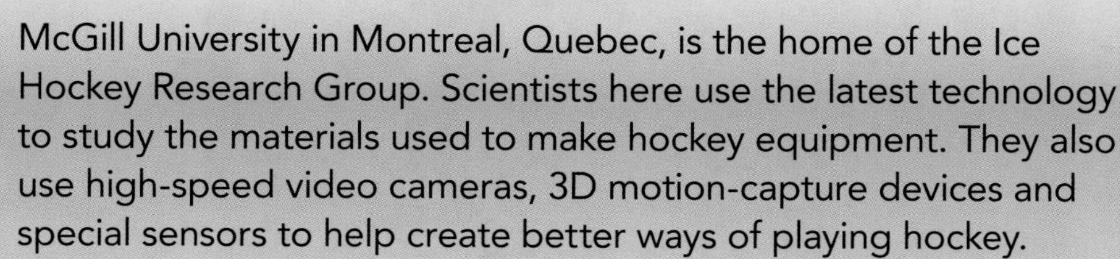

McGill University in Montreal, Quebec, is the home of the Ice Hockey Research Group. Scientists here use the latest technology to study the materials used to make hockey equipment. They also use high-speed video cameras, 3D motion-capture devices and special sensors to help create better ways of playing hockey.

9 THE PUCK STOPS HERE

Have you ever noticed that the pucks in an NHL game don't bounce as much as when you play? What is it about their pucks that makes this happen? Let's see.

You Will Need

- a friend
- several hockey pucks or rubber balls
- a freezer
- a hair dryer
- a metre stick
- a flat concrete surface

What to Do

1. Place one of the hockey pucks or rubber balls in the freezer for at least 2 hours.
2. Remove the puck from the freezer. Hold the hockey puck next to the top of a metre stick with the bottom of the stick placed on the ground. Drop the puck on its edge. Have a friend use the measurements on the stick to see how high the puck bounced.
3. Try this again, this time using a puck that is at room temperature. How high does this puck bounce?
4. Use a hair dryer to warm a hockey puck. When the puck is warm, drop it from the same level and see how high it bounces.

WHAT HAPPENED?

The frozen puck bounced the least, while the warmed puck bounced the most. Hockey pucks are made of rubber, which is very elastic, or flexible. When it is squeezed, it stores energy that can be released. The warmer the puck, the more energy it can store. When a puck hits the ground, it compresses and then expands, releasing its stored energy. This makes the puck spring back upwards. A warm puck will bounce unpredictably off the boards, so the NHL puts its pucks in the freezer before games.

10 RACING PUCKS

The harder you hit a hockey puck, the faster it will travel down the ice. Are there any other tricks to making a puck move faster? Let's see.

You Will Need

- an ice rink
- 3 hockey pucks
- 3 buckets or large bowls
- hot water
- room-temperature water
- ice water
- a towel
- a push broom

What to Do

1. Place each hockey puck into a bucket. Add hot water to the first bucket; add water that's at room temperature to the second; to the third, add ice water. Leave the pucks for a few minutes to allow them to reach the same temperature as the water.
2. Find a line on the ice to act as your starting line. Dry off the pucks with a towel and place all three of them side by side on the starting line. Make sure you know which is which!
3. Line up your push broom behind the three pucks and push it forward to shove all three pucks evenly down the ice. Stop pushing and note how far each puck travels. Which one moved the farthest?

WHAT HAPPENED?

After pushing the pucks along the ice, you found that the colder puck travelled farther than the warmer pucks. Cooling a puck down not only makes it bounce less (see "The Puck Stops Here," previous page), it also makes it slide better along the ice. Warmer pucks can cause the ice to melt as they travel along, and the wetness increases friction between the ice surface and the puck which slows down the puck.

11 MAKE YOURSELF BIGGER

In the classic novel, *Alice's Adventures in Wonderland* by Lewis Carroll, Alice drank a special liquid to make herself bigger. When you're a goaltender you don't have the option of sipping a special drink to become larger. What advice do you think coaches give goalies that will do the same thing?

You Will Need

- a helper
- a piece of construction paper
- a recipe card
- a pencil or pen
- scissors
- a ruler
- masking tape
- a plant mister

What to Do

1. Draw a 6 x 6 cm (2.5 x 2.5 in) square on the recipe card. Use scissors to cut out the square. This is your goaltender.
2. Draw a 7.5 x 7.5 cm (3 x 3 in) square in the middle of a piece of construction paper. This is your net. Use masking tape to attach the construction paper to an outside wall.
3. Fill a plant mister with water. Stand back about 1 m (39 in) from the wall, facing the construction paper, your "net." Have a helper hold the card, your "goalie," directly in front of the mister, as close as possible to you. Try spraying the net. All the water should hit the goalie, and none of it should hit the net.
4. Have your helper gradually move your goalie back toward the net as you continue to spray. Stop when the water just hits the edges of the net. Note the distance of the goalie from the net and from the sprayer.
5. Have your helper hold the goalie directly in front of the net as you spray. Note how much of the water hits inside the net.

WHAT HAPPENED?

You got more water on the net when the goalie was closer to it. But it was more difficult to "score" when the goalie was further out. This is what goalies do. They try to make themselves bigger by moving away from the net. This is called **telescoping**. By doing this, the goaltender cuts down on the number of angles a player has to shoot at the net. Ideally, the goaltender should be about halfway between the net and the player taking the shot. So why do goaltenders seem to stay close to the net if moving out helps them? There are several players on the ice and a quick pass could catch the goalie in the wrong position for a shot from another player.

COOL FACTS

The National Hockey League is always looking for ways to improve the game. In 2011 the league held a two-day research and development camp to test new rules and some new technology. In the 2011 pre-season, some of those things were tested, such as a net with clear plastic on top. This would make it easier to see if the puck crossed the goal line in video replays.

12 PLAY BALL

Lower body strength is important when it comes to racing down the ice, but hockey players also need a great deal of upper body strength to shoot, check and fend off aggressive checks from an opponent. Without using weightlifting equipment, is there another way to test the upper body strength of a player?

You Will Need

- a heavy ball or a large bag of rice
- a measuring tape
- a large, flat outdoor space
- a wall

What to Do

1. Sit against a wall so that your shoulders, head and hips touch the wall. Your feet should be straight ahead of you. Now spread your legs slightly so they form a V. Do not move from this position.
2. Have your helper hand you the ball or bag of rice. Hold it between your hands and move your arms so they are parallel to the floor with your elbows pointing away from your body. Your hands should be facing outward from your body. Make sure your hands are placed just above your chest, but lower than your neck. Keep your shoulders down.
3. Take a deep breath in and push your hands outward, releasing the ball or bag of rice. Do not move your back or hips away from the wall.
4. Have your friend measure the distance from the wall to where the ball or bag first hit the ground.
5. Try this three or four times. Can you make the ball or bag go farther the more you practise?
6. Try this activity again, but this time, allow your body to move forward as you throw the object. Did it go farther?

WHAT HAPPENED?

The ball went farther when you moved your body as you were throwing. This is because you used your back and stomach muscles as well as the muscles in your arms and shoulders. It was more difficult to throw the ball when you only used the muscles in your upper body. Using more muscles allowed you to throw the ball farther. This means you can exert a larger force or push as you throw the ball. **Power** is important for quick movements that require force, like throwing a ball or blocking a shot.

COOL FACTS

You probably know how to measure your height and weight, but did you know you can measure your **wingspan**? Hold your arms straight out from your body so your fingertips are as far apart as they can possibly be and have a friend measure the distance between your fingertips. Most people have a wingspan close to their height. The top NHL players can have wingspans over 2 m (6.5 ft). Having a large wingspan for your height allows you to reach farther for the puck.

13 VERTICAL LIMIT

The ability to jump high is obviously important for basketball players, but it's also important for hockey players. Strange, but true: one of the tests the NHL runs on players is something you'd expect to find in a basketball gym.

You Will Need

- an adult helper
- chalk
- a brick wall
- a flat space
- a measuring tape

What to Do

1. Rub chalk on the ends of your fingers. Stand next to the wall and, keeping your shoulders square, lift your hand up and touch the wall with your fingers. Leave a chalk mark to show how high you could reach. Use a measuring tape to measure from the ground to the height of the mark. This is your standing height measurement.
2. Rub more chalk on your fingers. Now stand in front of the wall and squat down slightly, pausing for a moment. Jump upward and touch the wall with your fingers, leaving a chalk mark. How high did you jump? Use a measuring tape to measure this height. Subtract your standing height measurement from this value. The difference is your **static** jump measurement.
3. Try this again, but this time squat all the way down and immediately jump upward to touch the wall. How high did you jump this time? Use a measuring tape to record this height. Subtract your standing height measurement from this value. The difference is your **counter-movement** jump measurement.
4. Keep practising both these jumps and see how your jumping height improves over time. Try swinging your arms downward as you squat, then throwing them upwards as you jump. Can you jump higher?

WHAT HAPPENED?

You jumped higher when you didn't pause before the jump. In preparing for the jump, you stored **elastic energy** in your muscles, which you were able to release as you jumped. This is similar to squeezing a spring and then releasing it. The NHL is very interested in a player's ability to make vertical jumps because it measures a player's power. When trying out for the league, players perform a similar test, except they use a machine instead of putting chalk on their fingers to record the height they jumped. Players get three tries and their best score is recorded.

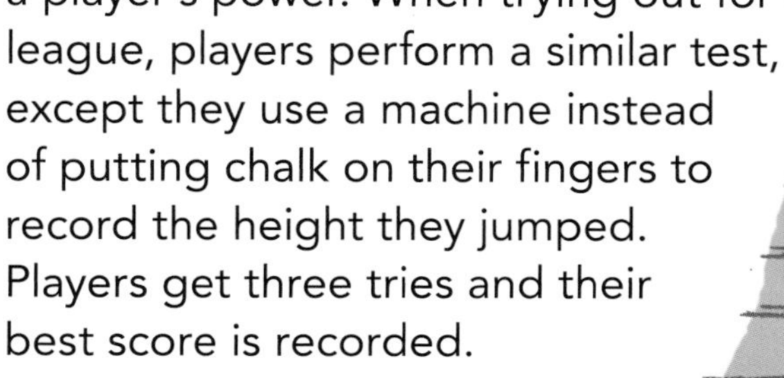

COOL FACTS

Power is a measure of the amount of work that can be done in a particular amount of time. When the **peak power** of an athlete is measured, it is measured in units of watts per kilogram. To estimate your power you can use the Sayers Formula. Multiply your jump distance in centimetres by 60.7. Then multiply your weight in kilograms by 45.3. Add these two numbers together then add 2055. This number is your peak power in watts. If you divide this number by your weight in kilograms that gives your peak power in watts per kilogram.

14 LONG JUMP

You're on a breakaway. How can you make sure you can stay ahead of everyone else? Believe it or not, you can practise jumping!

You Will Need

- a helper
- a measuring tape
- chalk
- a flat surface

What to Do

1. Find a flat area outdoors and use the chalk to draw a line. This is where you will do your jump.
2. Place your toes on the line and squat down, pausing for a moment. Jump as far forward as you can, landing on both feet. If you fall back, the jump does not count. Have your helper measure the distance you jumped. This is your static long jump.
3. Try this again, but this time place your toes back on the line and squat down, then immediately jump forward. Have your helper measure the distance you jumped. This is your counter-movement jump.
4. Keep practising and see if your distance improves.

WHAT HAPPENED?

You discovered that your counter-movement jump was farther than your static jump. Just as you saw in "Vertical Limit" (pages 26–27), storing elastic energy in your muscles made it possible to jump a greater distance. Not only do you have to have a high vertical jump to make it to the NHL, but you also need an impressive long jump. In fact, players in the NHL can propel themselves forward to distances of over 3 m (10 ft)!

15 IT'S JUST A JUMP TO THE LEFT

You now know that players have to be able to jump high and jump long distances, but what about jumping from side to side? If you've watched a hockey game, you know that players don't just skate straight down the ice. They have to move quickly from side to side to avoid an opponent or to control the puck. But what's the science in this?

You Will Need

- a flat surface
- chalk
- a measuring tape

What to Do

1. Find a flat area outside and use the chalk to draw a line.
2. Place your left foot along the line so the line runs along the inside of your foot. Lift your right leg. When you are ready, jump sideways to the right as far as you can. You must land standing up on your right leg. Mark where the inside edge of your right foot landed with chalk. Measure the distance between the lines.
3. Try this again, placing your right foot against the line and jumping to the left. Could you jump farther starting on your left leg or your right leg?

WHAT HAPPENED?

You found that you jumped a different distance for each leg. This is true with most people. It's harder to land doing this jump than the long jump, so you probably didn't jump as far. This activity is one where you mostly use your **fast twitch muscle fibres.** These fibres are like long strands of cells all connected together. The fast twitch fibres are what give athletes a burst of power. Your body uses these more when you are sprinting or playing hockey. Activities like distance running give your **slow twitch muscle fibres** a better workout.

16 IN-STABILITY

Standing on one foot sounds so simple. But it's harder than it seems. Balance, or the ability to stay upright on your skates, is obviously a very important skill for any hockey player. How can this activity help you stay steady on your skates?

You Will Need

- a helper
- a large cushion from a couch or a pillow from your bed
- a stopwatch

What to Do

1. Find a large empty space away from furniture, tables or windows. Shift your balance over one of your feet. Stand on one foot with your other foot lifted slightly off the ground. Use a stopwatch to time how long you can balance on one foot.

2. Try this again, only this time lift one foot off the ground and, once you are balanced, close your eyes. Have your helper start the stopwatch when your eyes close and see how long you can stay balanced.
3. Now, instead of standing on the floor, put a pillow or cushion on the floor and try standing in the middle of it. Does this make a difference to how long you can stay balanced with your eyes closed?

WHAT HAPPENED?

Balancing on one foot was hard. Using both feet gives you a more stable platform for balance. If you move your feet apart and bend your knees slightly, you will be even more stable. It was also easier to balance with your eyes open than it was when you closed your eyes. Your eyes used the horizon for clues to help keep you upright. Because it's soft, the cushion was an unstable surface. This made things wobbly in two dimensions — front to back and side to side. You had to constantly make small movements to keep yourself balanced. Your body began to fire many muscles in response to try to keep you balanced. This response is called "all or nothing." If you practised this, your body would become better at learning which muscles to fire and you would find this activity much easier. Hockey players use special balls or wobble boards to help them practise balance exercises.

COOL FACTS

The key to keeping balance is in your ears. Your inner ear has a group of three tubes called the semicircular canals. These tubes have tiny hair-like **nerves** and are filled with fluid. When your body changes position, the nerves are triggered and this allows your brain to tell you where your body is in space. If you have an ear infection it can affect your balance.

17 SNAKES AND LADDERS

What do hopscotch and hockey have in common? The thought of a big, muscular athlete playing hopscotch in the playground might make you laugh, but it could help his game. Fancy footwork, speed and concentration are all part of this next activity.

You Will Need

- a helper
- chalk
- a sidewalk
- a stopwatch

What to Do

1. Use chalk to draw a rectangle on the pavement about 45 x 450 cm (18 x 180 in) on the sidewalk. Divide the rectangle into 10 equal squares about 45 x 45 cm (18 x 18 in). Number the squares 1 to 10.
2. Stand on the left side of the first square. Place your right foot into square 1, then move your left foot into square 1.
3. Move your right foot to the right, out of square 1, and your left foot up into square 2.
4. Move your right foot into square 2 and then your left foot to the left, out of the square.
5. Move your right foot into square 3 and then your left foot into square 3.
6. Continue moving though the 10 squares following this pattern: one foot out, one foot in, both feet together.
7. When you have mastered the pattern, go as fast as you can and have a friend time you to see how long it takes you to complete the squares in both directions.
8. Now for the fun part. Once you are really confident about the pattern, have your helper run beside you as you go through the squares. Have him or her make noise, clap, yell or do anything to distract you. How fast could you run the squares with the distraction?

WHAT HAPPENED?

It took you some time and concentration to be able to run these squares using the correct pattern. It was harder to run the pattern correctly when your friend tried to distract you. You use a part of your brain near your forehead called the **prefrontal cortex** to concentrate. Sometimes you can concentrate so hard on one thing that you don't notice what is going on around you. But sometimes a distraction makes you focus on it instead of what you were focusing on in the first place. Even if you try to refocus, it takes a fraction of a second . . . enough to make the pattern harder to speed through. Players need to focus on their game and learn not to be easily distracted.

18 LAP IT UP

You might think you are in pretty good physical shape, but how do you think you compare to an NHL player when it comes to fitness? Obviously a professional hockey player can skate faster than you, but is that the only measurement? Let's see.

You Will Need

- a helper
- a running track
- a stopwatch
- water
- an apple (optional)
- a calculator
- a bottle of water

What to Do

1. Find a running track at a school or park. The track should be 400 m around.
2. Before the run, fuel your body with a few apple slices or other fruit, and a small glass of water. Have a water bottle handy.

3. When you are ready, have your helper give you a signal to start running. Have your helper start the stopwatch. See how many metres you can run in exactly 12 minutes.
4. Record your distance in metres. Subtract 505 from the distance you ran. Divide the answer by 45. This number gives you an estimate of your fitness level or VO_2 max in millilitres per kilogram per minute (mL/kg/min).

WHAT HAPPENED?

You ran a really long way in 12 minutes. The run you did is called the Cooper Test. This is one way to measure physical fitness. The calculation you did with your distance gives you an approximate value for your **VO_2 max**. VO_2 max is a measure of the ability of your body to use oxygen when you exercise. This tells trainers your fitness level. The average value for an NHL draft pick is around 56 mL/kg/min which means using this test they would be able to run about 3,000 m (1.9 miles) in 12 minutes. Of course, you can't compare yourself to an NHL athlete, only to someone your age.

COOL FACTS

During exercise, you change the sugar in your blood into a chemical called **lactic acid**. As your muscles begin to build up lactic acid, you will find that you can't continue to exercise at the same intensity. Different types of **muscle fibres** (see page 29) act differently with lactic acid. Using fast twitch fibres causes the lactic acid to form. So athletes like hockey players, who rely on fast twitch fibres for quick bursts of speed, have to rest and recover to be at their best. That's why players have shifts. Slow twitch fibres don't form lactic acid, instead they use it up.

19 THINK FAST!

Have you ever wondered how goalies make those lightning-quick glove saves? Of all the players on a hockey team, they're the ones who need those quick reflexes the most. But how is it possible for a goalie to position his body and place his equipment in just the right spot in time to stop a small object travelling at more than 150 km/h (93 mph)? How good are *your* reflexes?

You Will Need

- a helper
- a long wooden ruler or metre stick
- a table
- a hockey or goalie helmet (optional)

What to Do

1. Sit at a table with your forearm resting on it and your fingers reaching just over the edge. Spread your fingers and thumb 3 cm (1 in) apart.
2. Have your helper hold the ruler vertically between your fingers and thumb with the zero mark at the same level as your fingers. Don't touch or hold the ruler.

3. Have your helper release the ruler when he or she is ready. Catch it by pinching your fingers together. Do not use your whole hand to grab the ruler.
4. Record the mark where your fingers grabbed the ruler. Use the table below to see your **reaction time**.
5. If you have a helmet with a visor or cage, try this activity again while wearing the helmet. Did the helmet change your reaction time?

WHAT HAPPENED?

It may seem pretty quick, but in that short moment, a lot of things happened. First, light detector cells in your eyes sent a chemical message through your **optic nerves** to your brain. Cells in the **motor cortex** of your brain sent out an electrochemical message. This message travelled along a bundle of nerves in your spinal cord to **motor nerves** attached to the muscles in your hand. These nerves caused the muscles in your hand to contract and grip the ruler. The distance the ruler fell can be used to calculate your reaction time, shown below. How fast you are depends on many things, including your health, age and how tired you are. Try this experiment three or four times to see if you can improve your reaction time with practice.

Distance the ruler travelled	Reaction time
5 cm (2 in)	0.10 seconds
7.5 cm (3 in)	0.12 seconds
10 cm (4 in)	0.14 seconds
12.5 cm (5 in)	0.16 seconds
15 cm (6 in)	0.18 seconds
17.5 cm (7 in)	0.19 seconds
20 cm (8 in)	0.20 seconds
22.5 cm (9 in)	0.21 seconds
25 cm (10 in)	0.23 seconds
21.5 cm (11 in)	0.24 seconds
30 cm (12 in)	0.25 seconds

20 T-BALL

In "Think Fast!" (page 36) you measured your reaction time. In hockey, it's not just how fast you react; it's also how fast you move. How do you think hockey players train to think fast and move faster?

You Will Need

- 2 helpers
- 2 tennis balls
- chalk
- a large open area with a flat concrete or wooden surface

What to Do

1. Hold a tennis ball in each hand, then open your arms wide. Your arms and body should form a T.
2. Draw a line about 3 m (10 ft) away from you. Have 2 friends stand along the line so that each is in front of one ball. They should be about an arm's length apart from each other.
3. Make sure each friend is facing you and have them lie face down and flat on the ground with their arms next to their chest and their palms on the floor.
4. Wait a few seconds, then drop one of the tennis balls. When you drop the ball in your right hand, have the friend on the right side run for the ball and try to grab it before it bounces twice. When you drop the ball in your left hand, have the person on the left run for the ball.
5. Try this activity several times. If your friends find it too difficult to catch the ball, try moving closer to them.
6. When your friends can catch the ball dropped on their own side, switch it up. Have your friend on the right side catch balls from the left and your friend on the left catch balls from the right (but not at the same time!)
7. When both of your friends can catch the ball, take a giant step backward and see how well they do with a longer distance.
8. Change places with your friends and see how well you can catch the ball.

WHAT HAPPENED?

This experiment uses the vision and motor areas of the brain as well as muscles. Your friends may have found it quite difficult to catch the ball before the second bounce because it takes time for the sensory message to be sent from your eyes to your brain, for the brain to process the information and for the sensory message to be sent to your muscles. It also takes time to get up off the floor and move into position. It can be even harder when the ball is dropped on the opposite side. But practising this will improve their performance. Good hand-eye coordination is important in hockey. Hockey players have a split second to figure out where the puck is and to get to it or to shoot. The faster they can coordinate what they see with their movements, the better they will play.

21 WHAT'S YOUR ANGLE?

"A good hockey player plays where the puck is. A great hockey player plays where the puck is going to be." Those were wise words from "The Great One," Wayne Gretzky. Knowing where the puck is going is a major advantage. But rink ice isn't perfectly smooth. Pucks can collide with sticks, skates or the boards. In the real world, puck motion across the ice is chaotic; it changes dramatically with small changes in the angle and speed of the puck and with changes in the ice surface. If you could predict how the puck would bounce, how would you do it?

You Will Need

- a helper
- an asphalt or concrete surface with a solid wall
- sidewalk chalk
- a metre stick
- a protractor
- string
- tennis balls

What to Do

1. Using the metre stick and the protractor, draw a straight line at 90 degrees from the wall out about 3 m (10 ft). This is your normal line.
2. Stand at the end of the line and roll a tennis ball straight along the line at the wall. Watch how it hits the wall and bounces back. Try this again but roll the ball harder and faster at the wall. What happens then?
3. Now draw a straight line from the normal line at 45 degrees from the wall out about 3 m (10 ft).
4. Stand at the end of this line and roll a tennis ball straight along the line at the wall. Watch how it hits the wall and bounces back.
5. Have your helper hold one end of a string at the point where the ball hit the wall. Hold the other end where the ball ended its travel. Use the protractor to measure the angle the string made with the wall.
6. Once you have tried bouncing the ball at the 45 degree angle, try other angles to see how the ball travels when the angle is larger or smaller.

WHAT HAPPENED?

The harder you rolled the ball at the wall, the farther it travelled after bouncing. The amount of **kinetic energy** a travelling object has doesn't change when it hits a surface. When you rolled the ball at a small angle, it bounced back at a small angle. Rolling the ball at a larger angle made it bounce at a larger angle. What does this mean for hockey? It is often said that the boards around the arena are like extra teammates. When you shoot the puck at the boards, it bounces back at a specific angle. The angle that it bounces at is close to the angle at which the puck hit the boards. Good hockey players know the exact angle they want the puck to go and aim the puck for the perfect spot on the boards. What you thought was a smart play was really math on skates.

22 ODIFEROUS

When you play any sport, especially hockey, you can work up quite a sweat. The drippier you get, the more smell you seem to produce. You might smell better after a shower, but your equipment will still have the **bacteria** from your workout. If the smell coming from your gym bag is strong enough to peel the paint from walls, here's the activity for you.

You Will Need

- an adult helper
- 3 pieces of bread
- sealable plastic bags
- water
- a refrigerator
- a toaster
- a plate

What to Do

1. Spray a bit of water onto one piece of bread. Place the bread in a plastic bag and seal the bag. Put the bag in a warm spot, like a sunny window, and leave it there for a week.
2. Place a second piece of bread in a plastic bag and seal the bag. Put this bag in the fridge.
3. Have an adult lightly toast the third piece of bread and leave this bread on a plate on the counter.
4. Check each piece of bread after a week. Which bread has mould growing on it?

WHAT HAPPENED?

Mould grew on the moist bread that was in the bag and placed in a warm spot. The bread in the fridge and the toasted bread didn't have any mould. This is what happens in your gym bag. Bacteria, mould, and some other kinds of **fungi** love hot, moist environments. As you sweat, the sweat on your skin soaks into your clothes and equipment. Placing your dirty equipment into a gym bag, then sealing the bag, provides any bacteria or mould or fungus spores with the perfect conditions to thrive. The smell coming from your bag is simply the chemicals made by these **microbes** growing and decaying.

COOL FACTS

There are a number of things you can do to keep your equipment from smelling ripe. Make sure it is completely dry before storing it. Wipe down your equipment with an antibacterial product, then use a hair dryer to dry it. Don't store your equipment in the bag; hang it up in a cool place like a garage, so that it can air out. Charcoal, volcanic ash or other products can be used in your locker or gym bag to absorb odour.

23 EATING RIGHT

Hockey players need to eat and drink the right combination of foods to keep them strong and healthy. Sports teams have nutritionists who help players decide what they should eat. Players need to eat the right mix of nutrients and minerals. They need the mineral calcium to build strong bones. Let's look at what calcium does for your bones.

You Will Need

- 2 chicken bones of about the same size from a cooked chicken
- 2 glass jars with lids large enough to contain a chicken bone
- labels
- vinegar
- water

NOTE: Bacteria can grow on chicken so be sure to wash your hands and work surfaces with warm soapy water after doing this experiment.

What to Do

1. Make sure all the chicken meat is removed from the bones. Choose bones as close to each other in size and shape as possible.
2. Place each bone in a separate jar. Fill the first jar with vinegar and seal the lid. Label this jar "vinegar." Fill the second jar with water, seal it and label it "water." Leave the jars in a warm place where they won't be disturbed for three or four days.
3. Remove the bones from the jars and examine them. Try to bend the bones. What happens? How are they different from each other?

WHAT HAPPENED?

The chicken bone placed in the vinegar was easy to bend. The bone in the jar that contained only water was stronger and less bendable than the one in the vinegar. Vinegar contains water and a chemical called acetic acid that dissolves the calcium in chicken bones. Calcium is an important mineral for keeping your bones strong. And because hockey is such a physical sport, it's especially important for hockey players to have strong bones. You can get your calcium from milk, cheese and certain vegetables, such as broccoli.

COOL FACTS

Your body needs **carbohydrates** and **proteins** after a strenuous workout. Nutritionists recommend that you have some kind of carbohydrate, such as fruit or juice, within 30 minutes of exercising. This gives you more energy and helps to restore your levels of **glycogen,** the chemical your body makes to store carbohydrates for later use. Proteins from foods such as nuts, meat or milk give your muscles the **amino acids** they need to not only recover from the workout, but also to rebuild.

CHECK-MATE

When you watch a hockey game, you know what's going to happen when a big, heavy player delivers a clean check to a smaller player: most likely, the smaller player is going to end up on the ice. Let's see how the physics behind that check.

You Will Need

- a helper
- a flexible ruler
- a penny, a nickel, a dime and a quarter
- a tabletop with a smooth surface
- a pencil
- paper

What to Do

1. Grip the ruler firmly by one end. Hold one end 10 cm (4 in) from the edge of the table.
2. Place the quarter on the table so that it is about 2 cm (1 in) in front of the free end of the ruler. Pull back on the free end of the ruler to the edge of the table.
3. Using the other 3 coins as targets, place them on the table and shoot your quarter at each one. Have your helper measure the position of each before and after. Try each against the others and record your findings. Which coin moves the farthest?
4. Try using the quarter as the target and hit it with each of the other coins to see how far it travels.

WHAT HAPPENED?

You used the same force to propel your coin each time, but the distance the target coins travelled was different for each one because of the different **mass** of each coin. The heavier coin doesn't travel as far as the lighter ones. In hockey, if a heavier player hits a lighter one, the lighter player moves farther from the point of collision unless he digs in his skate blades and pushes back.

25 I'M SO TORQUED!

Hockey players can go fast — *really* fast. They can go up to 32 km/h (20 mph). When you watch them take off down the ice, they seem to be leaning forward. Can you lean that far forward without skating fast?

You Will Need

- a helper
- a protractor
- a wall

What to Do

1. Stand several centimetres away from a wall, facing it, with your feet about hip-width apart.
2. Lean forward and place your hands on the wall. Then walk your feet backward while you have your helper use a protractor to measure when your body is at a 45 degree angle to the floor.
3. Try to lift your hands off the wall without pushing.
4. Move closer to the wall and try again to lift your hands off the wall.
5. When you can move your hands off the wall and stand up, measure the angle your body formed with the floor.

WHAT HAPPENED?

You found that you had to move so that your body formed a larger angle with the floor in order to stand up. You can't lean forward at a 45 degree angle and stand completely still. When you skate, your body can stay at an angle that would normally cause you to fall over. You dig your skates into the ice and push backward. As you speed up, the forward acceleration of your feet allows you to lean forward at a much greater angle than you could if you were standing still. The only way you can stand at that angle without moving faster and faster forward on your skates is to lean on something, like the wall.

GLOSSARY

amino acids: a group of organic acids that combine to form proteins

ammonia: a colourless gas that has a strong odour

bacteria: tiny one-celled microorganisms; some bacteria are useful, but others can cause diseases

brine: a mixture of salt and water

carbohydrates: nutrients such as sugar and starch that provide energy

composite: a material that is made from several other materials

concussions: brain injuries that happen after a violent hit to the head

counter-movement: a movement in the opposite direction

elastic: material that can spring back to its original shape, size, or position after being stretched or squeezed

elastic energy: energy stored by the stretching or compression of an elastic material

energy: the ability to do work or to move an object

ethylene glycol: a chemical commonly found in antifreeze

fast twitch fibres: long thin pieces of muscle tissue used for quick actions for short periods of time

force: energy that changes the motion or shape of an object

friction: a resistance to motion of two moving objects or surfaces

fungi: members of a group including moulds, mildews and mushrooms that live on dead or decaying material

glycogen: the storage form of carbohydrates found in animals

kinetic energy: the energy of objects due to their motion

lactic acid: the organic acid formed in the muscles during exercise

mass: the amount of matter which can be measured

microbes: living things that are so small a microscope must be used to see them

motor cortex: the part of the brain that controls the movement of skeletal muscles

motor nerves: nerves that send signals from the brain or spinal cord to a skeletal muscle

muscle fibres: the long thin pieces of tissue that make up your muscles

nerves: fibres that can send an electrical impulse between the brain and spinal cord and the sensors and muscles of the body

optic nerves: the nerves connecting the brain and the eyes

peak power: the most power an athlete can exert measured in units of watts per kilogram

potential energy: any form of energy that is stored, such as the chemical energy in food

power: a measure of the amount of work that can be done in a particular amount of time

prefrontal cortex: the part of your brain just behind your forehead that you use to think and concentrate

pressure: the amount of force exerted on an area

proteins: essential nutrients made up of amino acids that are found in all animals and plants

reaction time: the time it takes your body to respond to a stimulus

slow twitch fibres: long thin pieces of muscle tissue used for endurance activities

static: not moving

telescoping: the action of the goalie moving away from the net to appear larger

VO_2 max: a measure of the ability of your body to use oxygen when you exercise

wingspan: a measure of the distance between the outstretched fingertips of your left hand and the outstretched fingertips of your right hand